# Praise for *Let's K.I.S.S.: Keeping Life Super Simple*

"Let's K.I.S.S.: Keeping Life Super Simple" by Dr. Tonya M. Hill is a refreshing and insightful guide that strips away the complexities of life, offering a clear and actionable roadmap to personal and professional fulfillment. As a reader who values clarity, effectiveness, and the power of simplicity, I found this book to be a treasure trove of wisdom that is both practical and profound.

I appreciated the fact that Dr. Hill's approach is rooted in her own life experiences, which she generously shares to illustrate the importance of core principles such as discipline, communication, and organization.

What sets this book apart is its ability to convey essential life lessons in a way that is both relatable and immediately applicable. Each chapter focuses on a specific life lesson, ranging from the importance of cultivating personal strengths to the value of creating lifelong friendships and the necessity of maintaining a strong financial plan.

As a leader, I appreciate how Dr. Hill underscores the importance of mentorship and a winning mindset—two elements that are crucial in both personal growth and leadership. Her emphasis on the power of verbal communication and the need to embrace and cultivate one's strengths resonated deeply with me. This book isn't just about personal development; it's a guide for anyone who wants to lead with authenticity and purpose.

The affirmations at the end of each chapter are a particularly powerful tool, reinforcing the lessons in a way that encourages the reader to internalize and apply them. Dr. Hill's writing is clear, concise, and infused with a sense of warmth and encouragement that makes the reader feel supported on their journey.

"Let's K.I.S.S." is a must-read for anyone looking to simplify their life and enhance their effectiveness, both personally and professionally. Whether you're a seasoned leader or someone just starting on their personal development journey, this book offers valuable insights that can transform how you approach your daily challenges and long-term goals. Dr. Hill's philosophy of "Keeping Life Super Simple" is a guiding light in a world that often feels overwhelmingly complex.

This book is a reminder that sometimes, the simplest solutions are the most powerful!

**—Derek Kenner, Ph.D.**

I've had the unique opportunity to witness both the personal and professional dedication that went into creating Let's K.I.S.S.. This book stands out as a crucial resource, offering life lessons that will resonate deeply with both students and faculty.

From an administrator's viewpoint, the practical and real-life applications of these lessons are what make this book powerful. This book is a call to action for improving our educational practices.

In short, Let's K.I.S.S. is a must-read that will inspire and impact students, faculty, and educational leaders alike. I am incredibly proud of Dr. Tonya Hill for creating a work that is as transformative as it is timely.

**—Marquis Hines, WI Hall of Fame Basketball Coach and Milwaukee Public School Principal**

EXCELLENT read!!! I took several nuggets away and reinforcements. I'll read again (and again, and again)!

**—Tonya Jones, Corporate Executive**

At the age of 54, I decided to write this book because I believe life lessons should be shared with those who desire to lead a productive joyful and fulfilling life. Several years ago there was a post on Meta that asked, "What advice would you have given your ten year old self?" After journaling the answer to this question, I realized that I have learned valuable lessons in my life that would definitely benefit others. That exercise sparked the idea of writing this book.

One lesson that I learned that I believe to be extremely valuable is that any idiot can complicate a situation. However, only those who have a great understanding of any subject matter has the ability to simplify an explanation of it.

Life can become complicated when we do not seek wisdom and understanding from those who have been able to flow through life with excellent results. In order to simplify our lives we just need to find people that are living the type of life that we desire and then duplicate their habits.

If you want to lead a joy filled life study the habits of joy filled people.

If you want to live an abundant life duplicate the habits of those who live a life of abundance. If you want to live a healthy life do what healthy people do. Let's K.I.S.S. is a guide to a simple and fulfilling life. I hope you enjoy it!

**Copyright © 2024 by Dr. Tonya M. Hill**

All rights reserved. No part of this publication may be reproduced, distributed, or transmitted in any form or by any means, including photocopying, recording, or other electronic or mechanical methods, without the prior written permission of the author, except in the case of brief quotations embodied in critical reviews and certain other noncommercial uses permitted by copyright law.

For permission requests, write to the author, addressed "Attention: Permissions Coordinator," at the email address below.

**Dr. Tonya M. Hill**
**drt@simplydrt.com**

Title: Let's K.I.S.S.: Keeping Life Super Simple by Dr. Tonya M. Hill.

Description: First edition. | Milwaukee, WI: Self-published, 2024

Cover design by Chaz Cotton
Interior design by Kotaro Kojima
E-published in United States.

This book is a work of non-fiction. All names, characters, businesses, places, events, locales, and incidents are documented as accurately as possible and are not products of the author's imagination. They represent real individuals, entities, and occurrences.

The author has used public records, personal interviews, and other verifiable sources of information to compile this work. Any resemblance to actual persons, living or dead, or actual events is intentional and is used with the understanding that all such details are factual.

# DEDICATION

**Jamison,**

This book is dedicated to you. God gifted me with a lifelong teacher when you were born. In your thirty-one years, you've shown me the true essence of patience, empathy, love, authenticity, and courage. Each day with you has taught me the importance of living in the moment, embracing joy, weathering every storm and creating anew.

Your unique journey has opened my eyes to a world of innocence and resilience that is often lost in adulthood. Through your eyes, I've learned to appreciate the small victories, the quiet moments of connection, and the boundless capacity of the human spirit.

You have faced countless challenges with an unwavering spirit, teaching me that strength comes in many forms and that we are all born with a definite purpose.

But above all, you've taught me the purest form of love. Your presence in my life has filled it with meaning and purpose. There is not one day that goes by without me thinking about and preparing for your future. You have shown me that love knows no boundaries and that it transcends words, actions, and circumstances.

As I dedicate these words to you, my dear son, know that you are the heart and soul of this book. Your spirit infuses every page with warmth, wisdom, and boundless love. Thank you for being my greatest teacher, my guiding light, and my source of endless inspiration.

I love you Jamie,
Mom

## CHAPTER 1 · LIFE LESSON #1

**Mom,**

For all the moments of quiet strength, for the countless times you held your head high and led with your heart, I thank you. You have been my guiding star, showing me not only how to endure but how to thrive with grace, dignity, and determination.

From you, I learned that love is a commitment—a choice made every day—and that true strength lies in kindness, compassion, and the courage to be authentic. Your wisdom and common sense have shaped me into the woman that I am. You taught me how to stand tall in the face of adversity, how to cherish life's smallest moments, and how to rise like a phoenix no matter the adversity.

Because of you, I know what it means to have support, to care with a full heart, and to always move forward no matter the circumstances. This book is a testament to the lessons you have woven into my life. Every word reflects the woman you raised me to be. I carry your love in everything I do, and for that, I am forever grateful.

I love you Mom,
Precious

# ACKNOWLEDGEMENT

**Marquis,**

From the moment you entered our lives, you embraced both Jamie and I with open arms and an open heart. Your spirit of kindness, patience, and understanding has created a haven for us, a place where we can truly be ourselves without hesitancy fear or judgment.

You have taught me the importance of compassion, offering not only your love to me but also extending it to my family. Anyone who can win the heart of my mother from day one has a special anointing! You have reminded us that together, we can overcome any obstacle that comes our way.

You have truly become an integral part of our family, and I am endlessly thankful for the love and support you continue to shower upon us.

I love and appreciate you.

Tonya

# BIO

**Title:** Let's K.I.S.S. Subtitle: Keeping Life Super Simple Author: Dr. Tonya M. Hill

**Background:** Dr. Tonya M. Hill's journey has been one of diverse experiences and remarkable achievements. Born and raised in Milwaukee, WI, she embarked upon a path of continuous growth and empowerment from a young age. Graduating from Rufus King High School at the age of 16, she pursued a degree in business administration at Marquette University, laying the foundation for her future endeavors.

**Entrepreneurship and Mastery:** Dr. Hill embraced entrepreneurship and motherhood in her early 20's. She ventured into the world of beauty as the owner of a boutique hair salon, where she honed her skills as a master stylist and became a freelance platform artist. Her passion for service led her to obtain a license as a COGIC minister, enriching her spiritual journey.

**Education and Recognition:** Driven by her commitment to personal and professional growth, Dr. Hill received her Doctor of Ministry degree from West Coast Bible College and Seminary in 2023. Her dedication to empowerment earned her a place on the Honorary Doctorate Degree Acceptance Program Committee, where she recognizes individuals making significant contributions to business and community.

**Network Marketing Expertise:** With over two decades of experience in network marketing, Dr. Hill has empowered thousands of independent business owners, generating over $75 million in sales with her former partner. Because of her leadership and expertise, she has been recognized multiple times in national business publications. She is a skilled trainer and mentor, guiding individuals to success in the network marketing industry.

**Forex Trading and Empowerment:** A certified trainer in the Forex market, Dr. Hill is passionate about equipping others with the skills needed for financial success. Through her expertise, she has helped countless individuals learn trading strategies to compound their trade accounts, believing that everyone should possess this valuable skillset.

**Community Engagement and Recognition:** Dr. Hill is a dedicated networker, connecting individuals to help achieve their goals. As a member and former president of Business Network International (BNI), she has played an active role in fostering business relationships and has been recognized as Networker of the Year by the Ohio Chamber of Commerce. Her commitment to safe networking events earned her recognition in Cleveland Magazine.

# BIO, CONT

**Soft Skills Training and Leadership:** As a Regional Vice President with Success Training Institute, Dr. Hill focuses on equipping students and professionals with essential soft skills. Her certification as a soft skills trainer reflects her dedication to meeting the high demand for these skills today.

**Passions and Superpowers:** Dr. Hill finds joy in learning, roller skating, music, fashion, fine dining, traveling, art and dancing. Her superpowers lie in adaptability and simplicity, driving her mission to simplify life's complexities and empower others to do the same.

**About the Book:** In "Let's K.I.S.S.", Dr. Hill shares insights and strategies for keeping life super simple, drawing from her diverse experiences and expertise. Through this book, readers will begin a journey of empowerment, learning how to embrace simplicity and unlock their full potential in every aspect of life.

The book cover features a clean and minimalist design, reflecting the simplicity and clarity advocated within its pages. With its compelling narrative and practical wisdom, "Let's K.I.S.S." is a guide to thriving in an infinitely evolving and increasingly complex world.

# SUMMARY

"Let's K.I.S.S.: Keeping Life Super Simple" is a book by Dr. Tonya M. Hill that summarizes her philosophy of leading a simplified and fulfilled life. Dr. Hill, a multifaceted entrepreneur, network marketing professional, success coach, and realtor, shares her insights and experiences in this book.

Through her journey from an entry level insurance professional to owning a boutique hair salon, becoming a licensed COGIC minister, excelling in network marketing, venturing into forex trading, and also a certified soft skills trainer, Dr. Hill emphasizes the importance of simplicity and adaptability in achieving success and fulfillment.

In "Let's K.I.S.S.," Dr. Hill offers practical advice and strategies for simplifying various aspects of life, from business and entrepreneurship to personal development and relationships. Drawing from her diverse background and experiences, she provides actionable steps and mindset shifts to help readers streamline their lives, overcome challenges, and achieve their goals with ease and joy.

This book serves as a guide for individuals seeking to simplify their lives, embrace their true potential, and find fulfillment in both professional and personal endeavors. Dr. Hill's superpowers of adaptability and simplicity shine through as she inspires readers to embrace simple life lessons as a pathway to success and happiness. She refers to this book as life's Cliff's Notes.

# TABLE OF CONTENTS

| | |
|---|---|
| **Preface** | 17 |
| **LIFE LESSON #1** | 19 |
| **LIFE LESSON #2** | 23 |
| **LIFE LESSON #3** | 27 |
| **LIFE LESSON #4** | 31 |
| **LIFE LESSON #5** | 37 |
| **LIFE LESSON #6** | 41 |
| **LIFE LESSON #7** | 45 |
| **LIFE LESSON #8** | 49 |
| **LIFE LESSON #9** | 53 |
| **LIFE LESSON #10** | 59 |

# PREFACE

A few years ago, a Facebook user posted the following question: "What advice would you give your 10-year-old self?" After pondering this question, I realized that my answers could help a lot of people. So, I decided to write this book. In this book I will share life lessons that I have learned over the years. I will provide you with very simple strategies that will help you avoid or remedy challenges that you will face during your life's journey.

I chose the title Let's K.I.S.S. because I love simplicity! "Keeping Life Super Simple" is what it stands for (the "I" in K.I.S.S. is a small letter L). For me, the more complicated a situation becomes, the more pain I associate to it, so I like to keep things extremely simple.

Do you remember your first kiss? I remember my first kiss. It happened while I was couple-skating at The Palace Skating Rink in Milwaukee, WI. It was in the early 80's. It was a simple kiss. There were no strings attached, no expectations, no pressures. It was completely innocent, and left me with a fond memory.

This book will offer you that same simplicity. My goal is to leave you with fond memories of lessons that you will be able to reflect upon and use for the rest of your life. By "Keeping life Super Simple," my prayer is that we all experience positive lives full of joy and fulfillment!

# LIFE LESSON #1:

## EMBRACE DISCIPLINE & ORGANIZATION

My favorite definition of the word "discipline" is "a system for rules of conduct." This definition resonates with me because it includes the term "system." System is an acronym for "Save Yourself Time, Energy, and Money." Every individual or entity that achieves success—whether a person, team, organization, family, business, church, or school—adheres to a meticulously designed system. Systems create order and order leads to the development of effective habits.

Similarly, my preferred definition of "organize" is "to arrange in a systematic way." Thus, when you combine the concepts of discipline and organization over time, success inevitably follows. A system of rules, methodically arranged, epitomizes both discipline and organization.

The significance of systems must be imparted to children both in educational settings and at home in order for them to create strong and beneficial habits. The lasting impact of implementing organized systems dawned on me when I began to observe that system-based thinking is the hallmark of some of the world's most successful leaders. As I reflect upon my upbringing, I am filled with gratitude for my parents and the countless sacrifices they made for our family. They passed on the lessons they had learned, laying down a solid foundation for me.

During my grade school years, my mother would wake up early in the morning, prepare herself for the day, and then wake me up to comb my hair before I dressed for school. My father, worked second shift, so he would take on the morning duties, preparing breakfast and driving me to school.

## CHAPTER 1 · LIFE LESSON #1

Quite often, I would arrive just in time or a few minutes late to school due to a lack of organization on my part. This routine, instilled by my parents, was my first encounter with a system, albeit one that highlighted my initial struggles with organization. Through these experiences, the seeds of discipline and organization were sown or lack thereof. Although I was taught a system it included both good and not so good habits. I remember feeling frustrated with my father for his leisurely driving as we headed to school, knowing very well that I'd be late. Yet, the source of my tardiness wasn't his driving; it was my disorganized morning routine. (Side note: Take full responsibility for all things. Never blame anyone else for things you can control).

After school, I rushed home to enjoy cartoons, outdoor play, or music. Homework and dinner were slotted in at some undefined time later. My homework station fluctuated between the kitchen table and my parents' bedroom, often accompanied by the background noise of a television. Bedtime was dictated by drowsiness rather than a set time. As I grew older, late-night phone conversations replaced sleep, leading to mornings marked by tiredness and a lack of focus in school.

Despite graduating high school early and securing a full scholarship for college, I now understand that discipline and organization could have propelled me further. This narrative describes the transformative power of systematic organization in developing positive habits from an early age. Had I grasped the significance of a scheduled routine for essential tasks and a designated area for my belongings, my daily life would have been smoother. More disciplined habits would have led to higher levels of performance in every area of my life.

## CHAPTER 1 · LIFE LESSON #1

Had I been more organized, my mornings would have started with making my bed and tidying my room, instilling a sense of order right from the start. After school, I would have diligently completed my homework at the kitchen table, carefully stored my work, ironed my clothes for the next day and placed my book-bag by the back door closet before diving into leisurely activities.

These simple yet effective habits, rooted in discipline and organization, would have created the building blocks for a more successful and focused life. This system would have paved the way for a balanced day, where fun and responsibilities would have coexisted. This approach embodies the importance of prioritizing necessities over pleasures. Embracing a responsible mindset, where the focus is on intentionally creating positive habits, while cultivating a life marked by happiness, confidence, and simplicity.

The practices we establish in our youth typically dictate the lifestyle we live as adults. Similarly, lacking organizational skills can stifle personal and professional advancement, productivity, and confidence. It's also a recipe for poor time management, anxiety, stress, and frustration.

Now, I invite you to take a moment for reflection. Identify areas in your life where discipline and organization could use a boost.

1.

2.

3.

# CHAPTER 1 · LIFE LESSON #1

Commit to bridging these gaps, aiming for a life that's not just lived, but fully experienced and enriched. Remember, the journey to a more organized and disciplined life begins with recognizing where we stand and envisioning where we wish to be.

**Develop Productive Personal Habits:**
1. Establish a morning routine: Wake up at a fixed time, make your bed, and allocate time for quiet reflection.
2. Prioritize self-care: Engage in prayer, meditation, visualization, affirmations, and exercise early in the day. You are your most valuable asset—looking after yourself enables you to care for others effectively.
3. Read 10 pages per day out of a personal development book.
4. Plan your mornings to avoid haste, incorporating time for dressing and unforeseen delays like traffic and parking.
5. Simplify meal times by preparing for the week on Sunday nights, ensuring a smooth, uninterrupted week.
6. Eat meals with your family to strengthen bonds and facilitate open communication.
7. Maintain a clutter-free and organized living space, including your home, garage, basement, closets, and car.
8. Keep a gratitude and aspirations journal, noting your thankful points, areas for improvement, and future desires.
9. Incorporate fun, laughter, and passion into every day, living life to the fullest.
10. Set meaningful and measurable goals.

**LIFE LESSON # 1:**
Embrace Discipline and Organization

**AFFIRMATION #1:**
I am disciplined and organized.

# LIFE LESSON #2:

## *HARNESS THE POWER OF VERBAL COMMUNICATION*

A solid definition of "communication" is "the effective transmission and exchange of ideas, emotions, and thoughts". The significance here lies in the term "effective." Effective communication enables us to articulate our feelings, needs, concerns, and seek the answers we require. It enhances our interactions, allowing us to ask pertinent questions that reveal the needs, emotions, and thoughts of those we have relationships with. Through successful communication, we uncover solutions and resolve the challenges encountered in our interactions. We are then able to develop trust, resolve conflicts, and cultivate enduring, healthy relationships.

Ineffective communication can cause disputes, breakups, resentment, decreased productivity, confusion, negative perceptions, disappointments, and eroded trust. I have experienced all of these negative consequences of ineffective communication. However, now that I know better I am able to avoid negative situations for the most part by simply choosing to communicate effectively.

As I think back upon my journey from childhood through my early twenties, I remember being shy and introverted. I believe this demeanor originated from a family environment void of encouraging dialogue and the expression of love through simple phrases like "I love you." It was not until I reached adulthood that expressions of love began to flow freely within our family. This shift in family dynamics led me to appreciate the importance of communication. When I was growing up my mom had a poem hanging on our kitchen wall.

I did not understand the significance of the poem until I had a child of my own. This poem embodies lessons that have since shaped my understanding and approach to sharing and connecting with others and here it is:

**"Children Learn What They Live"**
**by Dorothy Law Nolte**

*If children live with criticism, they learn to condemn.*
*If children live with hostility, they learn to fight.*
*If children live with ridicule, they learn to be shy.*
*If children live with shame, they learn to feel guilty.*
*If children live with encouragement, they learn confidence.*
*If children live with tolerance, they learn to be patient.*
*If children live with praise, they learn to appreciate.*
*If children live with acceptance, they learn to love.*
*If children live with approval, they learn to like themselves.*
*If children live with honesty, they learn truthfulness.*
*If children live with security, they learn to have faith in themselves and others.*
*If children live with friendliness, they learn the world is a nice place in which to live.*

In our home, for me, communication was synonymous with pain. My father, often under the influence of alcohol, would argue and belittle my mother, leading to instances of physical abuse. When this violence would occur, I would pray and ask God to stop the violence in our home. This pattern persisted from my early childhood until my senior year of high school, at which point my mother chose her peace and safety over staying in a turbulent environment.

## CHAPTER 2 · LIFE LESSON #2

My mother's response to my father's aggression was silence, a trait I found myself mirroring as it related to sharing my true personal thoughts and feelings. The shame of our family dynamics led me to retreat inward, seeking solace in solitude. Despite my prayers for peace, the violence continued, leaving me to question the efficacy of communication. If my heartfelt pleas seemed unheard by God, why would expressing my thoughts to others be any different? This experience shaped my perspective on sharing and communicating my feelings, embedding a deep sense of skepticism towards the act of opening up.

As my journey unfolded, God placed important people into my life who helped to reshape my view on communication. These friends and mentors freely shared their thoughts and emotions, positively impacting those around them significantly. One friend in particular, Wendy Davis, would express love to everyone she met. I remember challenging her genuine affection towards people with my skepticism. I would say to her, "You don't even know them. How can you love them?"

Now, at the age of 55, I understand the profound significance of saying "I love you." I've come to firmly believe our purpose, as human beings, is to love one another, embodying the spirit of Love itself. Thankfully, my journey has led me to openly share my emotions and inner most thoughts freely. I have embraced public speaking and I have been fortunate to have addressed audiences of ten's of thousands. Life's continuous evolution brings invaluable lessons. By integrating these lessons, we significantly enhance our life's quality.

*What aspects of communication do you find challenging?*

*What measures are you prepared to take for improvement?*

**Exercise Effective Communication by Mastering These Methods:**
1. *When speaking, adopt a friendly and non-intimidating tone with a smile .*
2. *Engage with questions without monopolizing the conversation.*
3. *Convey empathy through your facial expressions.*
4. *Establish a connection through eye contact.*
5. *Embrace written communication: leverage texts, emails, and other considerate methods for staying in touch.*
6. *Practice active listening to truly understand.*
7. *Utilize visual communication positively with pictures, emojis, and videos to enhance your message.*

**LIFE LESSON #2:**
Harness the Power of Effective Communication

***AFFIRMATION #2:***
I am a powerful and effective communicator.

# LIFE LESSON #3:

## *EMBRACE & CULTIVATE YOUR STRENGTHS*

Personal strengths embody the unique qualities and abilities that are inherently ours. Each of us is born with distinct talents, designed to be cultivated and offered to the world. Discovering and leveraging our personal strengths leads us to lives brimming with joy and fulfillment.

Discovering our personal strengths and unique qualities is best achieved through diverse experiences from a young age. I recall being introduced to a personality test in the late '90s, I was astounded by its accuracy! It made me wish that similar tests had been available during my school years so that I could better understand myself and more purposefully shape my future.

In grade school, my interests were broad and varied, encompassing math, spelling, jump rope, running, kickball, cycling, board games, basketball, drawing, fashion, modeling, roller- skating, tree climbing, fishing, traveling, and fine dining. I am naturally competitive and athletic, and I HATE to lose. Had I been more attuned to my natural talents, I might have chosen to pursue sports. However, from a young age, I opted to work, sidelining the opportunity to engage in athletics or extracurricular activities during high school.

For those of you with young children, it's crucial to observe and nurture their inherent skills. Exposing them to a broad spectrum of activities is essential for uncovering their talents. Focusing on these talents can guide them towards a rewarding life.

## CHAPTER 3 · LIFE LESSON #3

Tiger Woods' father dedicated time to nurturing his son's golfing talents, leading Tiger to achieve record-breaking success on the golf course.

LeBron James began his basketball journey at the age of 9. Recognizing the need for a more stable environment, his mother allowed him to live with a local youth coach, who introduced him to the game. Today, LeBron is celebrated as one of the greatest basketball players in history.

Michael Jackson's father guided him to concentrate on his performing talents, leading to his iconic status as the King of Pop.

I enjoy films based upon the true achievements of remarkable individuals. Recently, I watched a movie about Simone Biles, an extraordinary gymnast who won 11 Olympic medals so far. As a young girl, Simone moved in with her grandparents due to her mother's struggles with addiction. What might have seemed unfortunate turned into a pivotal moment. In the care of her grandparents, Simone found nurturing mentors and received focused training, which propelled her to become one of the greatest gymnasts in history.

"King Richard" is a compelling film that highlights the journey of Venus and Serena Williams, illustrating the power of personal strength. Raised by parents who valued discipline, organization, confidence, focus, and hard work, the Williams sisters were guided by their father, Richard Williams, who ensured they received top-notch coaching in tennis. Committed to their daughters' success, the family relocated to provide them access to the best training facilities. This strategic move placed Venus and Serena under the tutelage of elite coaches, setting the stage for them to become two of the greatest tennis players in history.

# CHAPTER 3 · LIFE LESSON #3

Imagine if the parents of the fore mentioned superstars hadn't recognized and nurtured their children's talents and needs. Their destinies would have been drastically different. Consider the countless individuals who might have led more fulfilling lives if they had only discovered their talents early on and been guided by mentors towards achieving greatness.

A clear understanding leads us to improvement. It's NEVER too late for GREATNESS, nor is it too late to support the young people in our lives in honing their natural born skills and talents.

*List the activities that bring you the most joy below...*

*Write out the things you have always wanted to pursue...*

Be courageous! GO FOR IT!

**LIFE LESSON #3:**
Embrace and Cultivate Your Personal Strengths

**AFFIRMATION #3:**
I am creating my best life now.

# LIFE LESSON #4:

## *FIND A MENTOR*

A "mentor" is defined as "an experienced and trusted advisor". Over the years, I've come to understand that a strong mentor significantly accelerates your path to success. From childhood, we learn through duplication and repetition. Our parents are typically our first teachers, guiding us through the basics like the alphabet and numbers. They nurture us and introduce us to colors shapes sounds and other essential knowledge. We observe and often imitate their actions, making our parents our initial mentors.

One invaluable lesson I learned from my mom is the importance of decorum, which encompasses behavior that reflects good taste and decency. My mom balanced a 9-to-5 job with selling real estate, all while managing our home, cooking meals from scratch, and sewing our prom dresses and other garments we needed or desired. Remarkably, I never once heard my mom swear, nor did she engage in smoking or drinking. She was adamant about my attendance at church as long as I lived under her roof—a demand I now look back on with appreciation. Reflecting on her influence, I see my mom as a paragon of decorum, embodying soft skills, common sense, work ethic, decency, perseverance, resilience, unconditional love, and strength. My mom remains an incredible mentor. I love you, mom; you are truly the best.

# CHAPTER 4 · LIFE LESSON #4

My father instilled in me the value of dreaming big. He would often share visions of building a home in the south, where he grew up. My dad was an entrepreneur at heart, a risk-taker, and for the most part a fun-loving father. From my dad, I learned how to count money, play cards, fish, drive, and cook. My knowledge about cars, the importance of travel, and the value of enjoying life also came from him. He exemplified what it meant to be a great provider, teaching me the significance of hard work and generosity. Rest well, Dad. I love you.

Growing up, my two sisters also served as my mentors. My love for music was inspired by my oldest sister, for whom music was a sanctuary. From my middle sister, I learned to appreciate nice things. She was always the most stylish in our home and acquired nice homes and cars at a young age. Surrounding ourselves with positive influences is crucial. We often adapt to our environments, so it's important to choose them wisely.

I hold immense appreciation for three high school teachers who have left a lasting impact on me. My typing instructor, whose skill I utilize daily, was exceptional in teaching the subject. My accounting teacher treated us as if we were her own children, setting high expectations and tolerating no excuses. Lastly, my French instructor transported us to France within the confines of his classroom. Fluent in the language, he encouraged us to speak French and carried himself with the elegance of a gentleman one might see in a Parisian film. He was intelligent, articulate, and moved with a sense of pride. My high school experiences were unforgettable, teaching me the value of striving for excellence. Generals for life!

I am eternally grateful for my first business mentor, encountered during my college years. At that time, I balanced two part-time jobs—one at an insurance company and the other at a hair salon. Working at the insurance company made me feel like a robot, as it didn't allow me to utilize my talents. In contrast, the hair salon was where I truly felt alive. The atmosphere was charged with positive energy, creativity knew no bounds, and meaningful relationships were forged. (I met my dear friends Lula and Cedric Mays at the salon back in the early 90's who are now like the sister and brother I never had.) There was a sense of ownership and freedom in the air at Tommy Arnez's place. Having always been a "hair girl," styling hair was one of my natural talents. I took pride in making sure my hair was always in place.

# CHAPTER 4 · LIFE LESSON #4

Starting as a receptionist at the hair salon, I seized the opportunity to learn more by asking the owner to mentor me in the business, to which he kindly agreed. Under his guidance, I learned the importance of a systematic approach in every aspect of the business, ensuring our clients received a professional and top-notch experience. He also imparted lessons on integrity, healthy eating, and spirituality. Progressing from an apprentice to a partner, I eventually gained the confidence and readiness to start my own business. Thanks to his exceptional mentorship, I was well-prepared for success. He was truly a phenomenal mentor.

The experience at the hair salon set the stage for the next chapter of my life. In 1996, I ventured into network marketing, a journey that has significantly shaped who I am today—and I'm just beginning. This path introduced me to numerous mentors who have enriched my life, both directly and indirectly. My time in network marketing has definitely been a personal development program, complete with its own compensation plan. The principle in network marketing is simple: the more you grow and help others to do the same, the greater your financial rewards. My first mentor in this field took great care to ensure I comprehensively understood the business. Along with her daughter, she held meetings on my behalf and offered the support I needed until I was capable of managing my business independently.

Over time, I encountered a gentleman from L.A. (Lower Alabama) who had crafted an enviable lifestyle for himself and his family. He upheld high moral standards in both his personal and professional life and demonstrated a strong, consistent work ethic. He became a model of excellence for me in the business, emphasizing the critical importance of making no excuses and the value of taking action. I absorbed every word he said and patterned myself in what I imagined his female counterpart would be. I mirrored his posture and overall approach to our business. Inspired by his example, I gained the courage and confidence to transition into a full-time network marketing professional in the fall of 1997.

## CHAPTER 4 · LIFE LESSON #4

In August of 2000, another pivotal mentor embraced me, imparting the critical lesson of connecting with a broad audience by conveying a universally relatable message. He schooled me in the arts of charisma, timing, and the crucial role of duplication in our business. Devoting countless hours to my development, he taught me the psychology behind our system. He also helped me to understand that our business plan is also our compensation plan, and that having a solid understanding of it is the first step to unlocking its full potential. From him, I learned the value of building connections with individuals from diverse backgrounds and the significance of embodying a servant leadership style.

He emphasized the significance of clear and impactful communication, helping me to realize that no one around me is more important or superior, encouraging me to embrace my personal power. He imparted the lesson that how we use our time will determine our success. After over twenty years of his mentorship, my focus has sharpened and I am committed to being TRUE—Transparent, Real, and Unedited. I am deeply thankful for the incredible mentors I've had, and those currently guiding me towards the fullest expression of my true self.

As we grow and mature, we ideally discover our passions and talents. Once we identify what we enjoy and our natural talents, the next step is to seek out at least one individual who has mastered the same skill and consider them a mentor. Emulate their practices diligently until you've honed the skill yourself. Then, infuse your unique flair to truly make it your own. If you're lucky, you may find mentors who are willing to invest time in your development personally. If not, take the initiative to find them. You can learn from reading books, watching movies, and biographies of great leaders. You can also make a list of the most successful people you know and get their permission to interview them. Ask them the questions that will unlock answers that will lead you to success. A mentor is a shortcut to your success.

## CHAPTER 4 · LIFE LESSON #4

A great mentor establishes a connection with you and strives to understand your unique qualities. They equip you with a proven system for success, essentially providing a blueprint to leverage your talents fully. Such a mentor holds you accountable, offering the necessary truth unapologetically. They challenge you to expand your boundaries, making room for personal growth and continuous improvement. A great mentor poses difficult questions, helping you to realize your inner strength. They offer encouragement through life's hurdles and lead by example, expecting you to hone your skills and eventually to mentor others. Thank you Dr. James Adlam and Dr. DL Wallace for being exceptional mentors.

Take a few minutes to identify the areas in your life that need improvement. Make a list of those areas below.


Now, write down the names of people who can mentor you in these areas whether through direct interaction or through indirect influence.


Finally, write a paragraph of what your life will look like once your mentors pour into you and after you take the necessary steps to be successful. THINK BIG!


**LIFE LESSON #4:**
Find a Mentor

**AFFIRMATION #4:**
I am committed to constant and never ending improvement.

# LIFE LESSON #5:

## *MAKE BIG THINGS OUT OF LITTLE THINGS*

The phrase "making big things out of little things" signifies the importance of slowing down to appreciate everything in life. The definition of "appreciate" is "to understand the worth or importance of something or someone and to admire and value something or someone". A mentor of mine often emphasized that anything above nothing is a blessing, reminding us that no one owes us anything in this world. Therefore, it's crucial to always show and express our appreciation and to practice gratitude in all areas of life.

Showing appreciation is fundamental, but equally important is the act of recognition. Recognition means acknowledging someone's presence and contributions, addressing a universal desire to feel appreciated, special, significant, and accepted. This highlights the importance of celebrating even the smallest acts, particularly in recognizing individuals for their efforts. Consider how we treat newborns, toddlers, or elderly family members.

When my son, Jamison, was a newborn I was exceptionally attentive and protective. I was also a nervous wreck because I had no idea what to expect as a mom with this precious newborn. I remember spending hours sanitizing our home before he was born. I wanted everything to be perfect and safe for him. After we brought him home, I remember the daily nurturing activities that my son experienced: he was held, rocked to sleep, sang to, bathed, read to, fed, changed and hugged among other things.

# CHAPTER 5 · LIFE LESSON #5

An article in Psychology Today highlights the critical importance of physical affection for infants, noting that babies who lack sufficient holding, hugging, and comforting can experience stunted growth and, in severe cases, may even face death. When it comes to toddlers, parents celebrate even the smallest milestones with great enthusiasm. Whether it's a toddler taking her first step or uttering "mama" or "dada" for the first time, these moments are met with an outpouring of praise, laughter, cheers, and applause.

Consider the care given to an elderly person who is no longer able to look after themselves independently. My mother just celebrated her 84th birthday and we are blessed to still have her with us. Her mind is good but her body is not what is used to be. So, we naturally adopt a demeanor of patience, empathy, and love. Our steps are slower to match her pace, our voices rise to meet her hearing, and we listen to her repeated stories as if it were our first time hearing them. Ensuring that our loved one receives the best possible care becomes our utmost priority.

Making big things out of little things is crucial, regardless of a person's age. Simple words like thank you or I am proud of you go a long way. Teenagers, adults, and seniors all deserve our care, concern, empathy, respect, and love, as they/we are precious and fragile too. It's essential to celebrate our loved ones; embrace the practice of hugging your family and friends daily, expressing your love and appreciation for them. Notice the small details that matter to them, perhaps surprising them occasionally with a thoughtful gesture like their favorite beverage, snack or a gift card to their favorite restaurant. Regular phone calls to your loved ones to share your thoughts and love are invaluable. Greet everyone with a smile, make eye contact, and turn complimenting others into a routine.

Recognition is so powerful that there's a saying, "babies cry for it and men die for it." By valuing the small moments, you make significant, lasting impacts. I've learned from personal experience, having once been so engrossed in work and myself that I inadvertently made my closest loved ones feel undervalued and unappreciated. This is a mistake to avoid. My journey has taught me the profound importance of making big things out of little things.

## CHAPTER 5 · LIFE LESSON #5

*List the names of the people closest to you below.*

*Identify some of their favorite things below.*

*Consider actions you can take regularly for each person to express your love and appreciation. Begin with the simple yet impactful act of regularly telling them how much you love and value them. Surprise them with some of their favorite items and always ensure your actions are sincere.*

Now make a list of things that make you feel loved and appreciated.

Request permission from your loved ones to share the things that make you feel loved and appreciated. Taking a deliberate approach in our closest relationships can make a significant difference.

**LIFE LESSON #5:**
Make Big Things out of Little Things

**AFFIRMATION #5:**
Everyone is significant.

# LIFE LESSON #6:

## CREATE LIFE-LONG FRIENDSHIPS

My preferred definition of a "friend" is "a person with whom you share a mutual bond of affection and support unrelated by blood and without any sexual relationship".

Take a moment to remember your first best friend. If you're still close with them, it's likely you learned the importance of cherishing your relationship from a young age. Maybe you both made deliberate choices to stay connected, like attending the same schools, going to the same church, sharing hobbies, or making a pact to always stay best friends—and you've kept that promise. Lifelong friendships are vital to our well-being, offering a sanctuary for open, judgment-free communication. A best friend enriches your life with anticipation for calls, outings, trips, and holiday traditions. Your best friend is someone who aligns with your interests and values, understands your preferences, and makes you feel valued in this magnificent world we live in.

My first best friend lived just two doors down from my childhood home, and we were born nine months apart. Upon bringing me home from the hospital, my mother recounts that my best friend's mother expressed a desire for a little girl of her own, leading to my best friend's birth nine months later. From my earliest memories, we were inseparable—playing, sharing secrets, celebrating holidays and birthdays together. We spent nearly every day in each other's company. Whenever she left for family visits to Georgia during the summer, I eagerly awaited her return.

## CHAPTER 6 · LIFE LESSON #6

During our junior high years, we explored the city of Milwaukee on our bikes, embracing every adventure. Without the luxury of cell phones or GPS, we mastered the art of navigating through streets with only signs and maps to guide us. Those journeys were filled with laughter and discovery. The era of boom boxes brought us together in a new way; we'd sit outside, soaking in the music, recording our favorite songs onto cassette tapes to create our own personalized playlists. We even coordinated our outfits and hairstyles, blurring the line between friends and family.

As we aged, our paths separated due to differing interests. We attended rival high schools and found new circles of friends who shared more in common with us individually. Thus, after the first 12 years of my life spent with a singular best friend, we gradually drifted apart.

When I was 16, I started my journey at Marquette University. During freshman orientation I encountered PT who quickly became a guiding figure in my life. He made me feel welcome and introduced me to the vibrant college campus life. PT and I shared an immediate connection.

PT and I discovered that we enjoyed the same food fashion and music, though he had a love for gospel, which I had not embraced at that age. We resided in the same coed dorm during my first two years at Marquette, West Hall. During that time our friendship blossomed. I would cook elaborate meals in our dorm with a hot plate, that I was not supposed to use in my room, much to PT's delight. Occasionally, my culinary ventures would trip the power on our dorm room floor due to the hot plate's high wattage, we would find ourselves in the dark with no power lol. PT worked at a video store so we expected him to bring home a selection of movies and popcorn for our late-night viewings, creating countless memorable moments.

## CHAPTER 6 · LIFE LESSON #6

Our shared passion for fashion led us to frequent shopping sprees at the Grand Avenue Mall, a bustling hub in downtown Milwaukee at the time. We prided ourselves on having an eye for fashion you couldn't tell us we weren't SHARP! Additionally, PT dedicated his time to working at a shelter for troubled teenagers. Remarkably, he balanced three jobs, maintained full-time enrollment at Marquette University, and achieved academic success, a testament to his extraordinary commitment and capability.

PT and I share a UNIQUE understanding of one another; we've never experienced a fallout, harbored anger towards each other, or turned our backs on one another for any reason. Since the summer of 1986, he has been my unwavering best friend, standing by me through all of life's significant events—serious relationships, birthdays, marriages, the birth of my son, divorces, and beyond. We are not just friends but also business partners who have traveled the world together. The beauty of our friendship is that we expect nothing from each other yet we know we can count on each other for just about anything.

PT embodies loyalty, love, kindness, generosity, thoughtfulness, empathy, and responsibility—he truly represents what it means to love. A world filled with friends like PT would indeed be a utopia. Surrounding yourself with people of such quality, filled with love and integrity, undeniably blesses your life. The only constant in my life longer than PT has been my 84-year-old mother. My gratitude for PT's steadfast friendship knows no bounds; he is indeed my ultimate ride or die and the brother I never had.

I hope everyone finds a PT in their life, as lifelong friendships are invaluable. According to an article by the Mayo Clinic staff, here are the benefits of adult friendships: they enhance your sense of belonging, elevate happiness, diminish stress, bolster self-confidence and self-worth. They play a crucial role in navigating through life's traumas, such as divorce, the death of a loved one, serious illnesses, and job losses. Furthermore, strong friendships motivate you to adopt healthier lifestyle choices, steering away from excessive eating, drinking, and sedentary habits.

## CHAPTER 6 · LIFE LESSON #6

Nurture your lifelong friendships if you're fortunate to have them. For those seeking such bonds, be open to forming new connections whether you're at school, work, community events, volunteering, or indulging in your favorite hobbies. Embrace positivity and approachability to radiate a welcoming vibe. Express genuine interest in others to naturally attract people who want to connect with you. Above all, embody the qualities of the friend you wish to meet.

*What key qualities do you look for in a best friend?*

*How can you enhance your personal development to fortify your bonds with lifelong friends?*

*Describe how these enhancements will create a stronger bond between you and your friends.*

*Write briefly about a moment when your best friend was there for you that you appreciated and then remind them of how grateful you are because of it.*

**LIFE LESSON #6:**
Create Life-Long Friendships

**AFFIRMATION #6:**
I attract quality people into my life!

# LIFE LESSON #7:

## CAREFULLY ENTER INTO INTIMATE RELATIONSHIPS

Let's simplify a complex topic by defining "intimate" and "relationship." I understand "intimate" to mean a deep connection, while "relationship" refers to how two people interact. Often, the term "intimate relationship" conjures images of a couple sharing a bond that includes sexual intimacy. This was once my view, until wisdom and awareness expanded my understanding. Today, I believe that while sexual intimacy can occur between any two people, the true essence of an intimate relationship lies in shared core values, mutual respect, ongoing encouragement, trust, consistency, optimism, growth, harmony, and support.

Based upon the definition above I have had intimate relationships with my family members friends mentors teachers and former husbands. When I think about my first best friend that I mentioned earlier I understand now that we shared an intimate relationship void of sexual relations until we grew apart. I had friends in grade school who I talked to daily and visited outside of school hours we had intimate relationships at the time without having sexual relationships.

I remember my first real boyfriend. Reflecting on this first significant relationship, I understand now why our bond was so powerful. We shared core values, enjoyed similar interests, and relied on each other completely. We were best friends, inseparable throughout high school, unwilling to spend a day apart. However, as life unfolded and new experiences came our way, our paths separated. Our interests evolved, we met new people, and eventually, we went our separate ways. Despite this, our connection endures, rooted in a genuine love for one another. We now view each other as family.

## CHAPTER 7 · LIFE LESSON #7

Conversely, there are times when relationships are primarily founded on sexual encounters. Often, when such relationships conclude, one or both individuals may regret investing their time and physical intimacy in someone who didn't truly respect appreciate nor love them. While I don't claim to be an expert on intimate relationships, I can share insights from over 40 years of personal experience.

**Tip #1:** Cultivate a deep and intimate relationship with yourself. KNOW THY SELF and TO THINE SELF BE TRUE! Discover your true essence. What are your core values? Explore your spiritual beliefs. How do you define respect? What qualities are important to you as you establish intimate relationships? Never compromise your beliefs and values. Consider your life's ambitions: do you envision traveling the world before settling down, or is starting a family first on your agenda? Reflect on your desire for children, the priority of your career versus family life, and your stance on marriage.

**Tip #2:** Reserve physical intimacy for someone you intend to commit to long-term. In my opinion this is crucial due to the spiritual connections formed through sexual intercourse. Consider whether you wish to be spiritually bonded with this person for a lifetime. Also, you have one precious and sacred body. Think about how protective you would be with a new born baby. You would be very particular about who you would entrust with your baby. I believe we should be just as particular with ourselves no matter what the age or circumstance. If you don't see yourself as invaluable no one will.

# CHAPTER 7 · LIFE LESSON #7

Build a strong foundation for your life, aligning closely with your truth and values. This alignment will guide you in forming meaningful intimate connections. Stay true to yourself when you meet that special someone. Both partners should enhance each other's best qualities. Do not suppress your voice, talents, gifts, or desires for the sake of a relationship; doing so may lead to losing your true self and happiness. Avoid trying to change others to fit your preferences, and resist altering yourself for someone else, as such efforts are futile. The aim for many is to lead a life that's transparent, real and unedited filled with joy, fulfillment, and happiness. Prioritize yourself, embrace your authenticity, and you'll attract the right people. Material possessions like money, homes, cars, and vacations will come and go, but true connections endure for a lifetime.

*Reflect on your relationship with yourself. What are the core values and beliefs that define you?*

**NEVER COMPROMISE YOUR TRUE SELF FOR SOMEONE ELSE!**
INVEST IN YOUR PERSONAL GROWTH AND AMPLIFY YOUR EXISTING QUALITIES.

**LIFE LESSON #7:**
CAREFULLY Enter Into Intimate Relationships

**AFFIRMATION #7:**
I am enough. Everything else is a bonus.

# LIFE LESSON #8:

## *YOUR HEALTH IS YOUR WEALTH*

In the year 2000, I began a regular workout routine. Despite understanding the importance of physical fitness and healthy eating, I often find myself needing to muster the motivation to follow through. The thought of what I could lose if I neglect this habit—such as my health, longevity, and dress size—drives me more than the gains. Interestingly, we are often more compelled to act by the potential of loss than by the promise of gain. Throughout my journey towards better health, I've discovered valuable insights that I'm eager to share, hoping they'll assist you as well.

Choosing a time that fits into your schedule and dedicating at least 30 minutes to exercise five days a week can be a game changer for your health and wellbeing. It's not just about penciling it in; it's about making a commitment to yourself. Mixing up your routine with yoga, weight training, and cardio ensures that you're not only working on flexibility and strength but also boosting your heart health. Think of it as your personal blend of physical activities that keeps things interesting and prevents monotony. It's like giving your body a surprise party of movements that it will thank you for later in life.

Keeping your ideal weight in check might sound like a challenge, but here's a simple yet effective strategy: divide your day into segments—eat within an eight- hour window, dedicate another eight hours to restful sleep, and spend the first and last four hours of your day fasting. Imagine this as your daily cycle, a rhythm that your body gets to groove to. During those fasting periods, it's not about denying yourself but rather, nourishing your body in a different way. Sip on alkaline water and green tea; think of them as your liquid allies, flushing toxins and keeping you hydrated, while you give your digestive system a well-deserved break. This isn't just about weight management; it's a holistic approach to living healthier. Your body gets the time to reset and recharge, akin to giving your system a daily mini-vacation. So, embrace this rhythm, and you may find yourself not just at your ideal weight, but also enjoying a newfound sense of vitality and wellness.

## CHAPTER 8 · LIFE LESSON #8

When it comes to fueling your body during your eating window, think of clean eating as your mantra. Picture your plate filled with vibrant fruits, crunchy nuts, and fresh vegetables—foods that look good, taste good, and do good for your body. And if meat is part of your diet, remember that how you cook it matters. Grilling or baking instead of frying not only keeps the flavor but also ensures you're eating healthier. But hey, we're all unique, and what works for one might not work for another. That's where a little professional guidance can be a game changer. Don't hesitate to reach out to your healthcare provider to craft a meal plan that's just right for you. It's not about following a one-size-fits-all approach; it's about finding what suits your body and lifestyle. So, embrace the journey of eating clean, and watch how your body thanks you in its own special way—with more energy, clearer skin, and a happier you.

Drinking eight glasses of water a day might seem like a tall order at first, but think of it as your daily hydration goal. Imagine each glass as a step towards flushing out toxins, keeping your skin glowing, and ensuring every cell in your body is happily hydrated. It's like giving your body a consistent flow of nourishment throughout the day. You don't have to chug all eight glasses in one setting; spread them out, making each sip a refreshing break.

Steering clear of white sugar, white flour, white potatoes, white rice, and white pasta can be a game-changer for your diet. And while you're at it, waving goodbye to dairy, corn, and processed foods can open up a new world of eating habits. Think of it as decluttering your diet, making room for more colorful, nutrient dense foods that not only taste great but also do wonders for your body. It's about choosing to nourish yourself with foods that support your health and wellness goals.

Giving your body a regular detox can feel like hitting the reset button. Herbal teas and natural supplements that target the colon, liver, kidney, and bladder can work wonders in flushing out toxins and keeping your systems running smoothly. It's like a spa day for your insides, leaving you feeling refreshed and rejuvenated. So, why not make it a habit to cleanse and care for your body from the inside out?

# CHAPTER 8 · LIFE LESSON #8

Making exfoliation a part of your routine is like giving your skin a new lease on life. Dry brushing before you shower, followed by indulgent massages, manicures, pedicures, facials, and body scrubs, can not only enhance your skin's health but also boost your overall sense of wellbeing. It's your personal time to pamper and care for your body, celebrating all that it does for you.

Keeping up with regular physical exams and dental check-ups, along with annual vision and hearing screenings, is like doing regular maintenance on your most precious vehicle—your body. These check-ups ensure everything is functioning as it should and can catch any potential issues early. It's about investing in your health now to enjoy the benefits long-term, ensuring you stay in top shape to enjoy all life has to offer.

Jumping on a rebounder for cellular exercise is not just fun; it's also an incredibly effective way to keep your body in shape. It strengthens your muscles, improves your balance, and enhances your cardiovascular health, all while being gentle on your joints. It's a joyful, low-impact workout that packs a punch, making fitness something you look forward to every day.

Finding an activity that fills you with joy and helps you burn calories is like hitting the jackpot of healthy living. Whether it's skating, dancing, hiking, swimming, or cycling, when you love what you're doing, it doesn't feel like exercise—it feels like play. Engaging in your favorite activity as often as possible is the secret to staying active without it feeling like a chore. It's about blending joy with movement, turning fitness into a celebration of what your body can and wants to do.

A well-known Book reminds us that our body is our temple, a unique gift that we're responsible for maintaining. Treat your body as you would anything of TREMENDOUS value.

# CHAPTER 8 · LIFE LESSON #8

*What are a few things you can do to improve your daily food and water intake?*


*Are you at a healthy weight? If not, what activity do you enjoy that you will do more of to improve?*


*When was your last physical exam? Be sure to get your body checked out and regularly maintained. It is definitely our temple.*


**LIFE LESSON #8:**
Your Health Is Your Wealth

**AFFIRMATION #8:**
I am deeply thankful, appreciative, and grateful for my precious body.

# LIFE LESSON #9:

## STICK TO A STRONG FINANCIAL PLAN

Money ranks alongside oxygen as a necessity for living, especially in a capitalistic society where freedom is closely tied to financial resources. Contrary to the notion that money is the root of all evil, it serves as a tool for securing our survival needs and fulfilling our desires. Like any tool, its use depends on the hands that use it. With this perspective, let's delve into the topic of personal finance.

The five key pillars of finance are creating income, wise spending, consistent saving, strategic investing, and protecting your assets. While I am not a financial advisor, I offer insights from my personal learning and experiences. My initiation into personal finance began when my father started giving me an allowance. He would hand me $20 each week, advising me to save half and spend the other half as I wished. As I grew older, this allowance increased to $40 per week until I took on a part-time job, at which point the allowances ceased. Over time, I came to believe that increasing my earnings meant working more hours or securing a second job. As my financial IQ increased I learned the value of incorporating the efforts of other people.

In high school, I worked in a file room at a community hospital, organizing charts after school hours. During college, I workeded two part-time jobs—one at an insurance company and the other at a hair salon. While pursuing an undergraduate degree in business, I noticed that the curriculum was designed not to prepare us for wealth and business ownership, but rather to prepare us to be employees.

# CHAPTER 9 · LIFE LESSON #9

When I first started working for a major insurance company I was excited! I believed that the possibilities would be endless. However, over time I felt like I was being extremely undervalued and robotic. I was just a number. I witnessed office politics nepotism and racism. It did not take me very long to understand that I was not meant to be molded into corporate america as an employee. I did not feel free and the income potential with my credentials were not very impressive.

In contrast, when I worked at the hair salon, I would count the day's earnings from the cash register and get extremely excited! In addition, the salon owner, who also became my first business mentor, enjoyed the freedom of setting his own schedule, engaging in creative activities throughout the day, educating his clients about hair care, and making them look beautiful.

Eventually, I asked the owner if he would teach me the business and he agreed. In 1991, I began the Cosmetology Apprentice Program at Milwaukee Area Technical College. My schedule consisted of theory classes on Mondays and hands-on training under my mentor's guidance from Tuesday through Saturday. I liked the idea of earning while learning. That was a great upside of the apprenticeship program.

My passion for hairstyling dated back to childhood, from intricately braiding and beading my god sister's hair to rolling my mother's hair at night. In high school, my unique styles and haircuts earned me the title of 'best hair' from my senior class. Pursuing a career as a stylist was a natural fit, allowing me to turn a natural talent into a profession with the entrepreneurial freedom and limitless earning potential I desired.

My first mentor emphasized the importance of client education. We advised them on the best daily hair care products and demonstrated how to shampoo and style their hair at home. Our objective was to reserve our schedule for professional services, such as precision haircuts and chemical treatments, that required our expertise. Additionally, we sold retail products, enabling clients to maintain their hairstyles between visits. We always scheduled their next professional appointment before they departed, with most clients booking a standing visit every six to eight weeks.

# CHAPTER 9 · LIFE LESSON #9

We maintained timeliness, professionalism, and a serene atmosphere, which naturally attracted clients who valued and mirrored these qualities. Our approach to every aspect of the business was intentional, professional, and systematic.

Over time, my mentor presented me with an opportunity to become his partner and prepared me to be a platform artist, enabling me to travel to cosmetology events and earn significant fees for just an hour or two of work. In my early 20s, I was thrilled by the income I generated as a stylist, benefitting from three revenue streams: client appointments, product sales, and platform appearances. By my late 20s, I was in a very comfortable financial position. I was free from debt, with significant investments no student loans, a homeowner, and the owner of a sleek red sports car.

In 1996, I ventured into the network marketing industry, discovering the power of working smarter by creating residual income, in addition to my career as a professional stylist. Residual income allows you to perform a task once but continue earning from that effort as long as your customers pay for the services you offer. By November 1997, I chose to dedicate myself to network marketing full-time, scaling back on client appointments to allocate more time to growing my network marketing business—a decision that proved to be incredibly rewarding.

In 2000, I partnered with someone who played a crucial mentoring role in my life as we built a thriving business together, generating over $75 million in sales and enjoying an exceptional lifestyle. We indulged in material luxuries, traveled globally, gained national media attention, and fostered a business environment that felt like an extended family. Although our personal paths eventually parted, I value the experience immensely. Those two decades equipped me with the knowledge and skills to build an even more prosperous financial future for myself.

Blessedly, I have continued to thrive as a network marketing professional and I am just scratching the surface of where I will be financially. I shared my journey with you so that you would understand the importance of securing exceptional mentors eager to guide you towards success. As a result of my mentors pouring into me I believe that it is my duty to mentor others, ensuring a brighter future for the coming generations. Throughout my network marketing adventure, I gained invaluable insights into personal finance, significantly influenced by my distant mentor, Robert Kiyosaki, the acclaimed author of Rich Dad Poor Dad.

I strongly suggest reading it if you haven't already. At the book's conclusion, the author promotes for his readers to play the board game Cash Flow, designed to instruct players on wealth accumulation. In this game, each participant receives an occupation along with a corresponding income statement.

The object of the game Cash Flow is to generate sufficient passive income—earnings from businesses and investments—to surpass your monthly expenses. Achieving this milestone paves the way to pursuing your ultimate dream, whether it's traveling the globe, creating a stock market for kids, running for mayor, or experiencing the 7 wonders of the world. Victory in the game is achieved by either landing on your dream with enough funds to afford it or by boosting your passive income by $50,000. This game offers a practical blueprint that anyone capable of reading and adding can apply to attain financial independence in real life. If you haven't read Rich Dad Poor Dad or played the Cash Flow game, I highly recommend you do so without delay.

Establishing multiple reliable income streams early in life is advisable. Cultivating the habit of spending 50% on needs 30% on wants saving 20% of your monthly earnings is a simple responsible budget plan. I recommend setting up four accounts: the first for retirement, untouched until you retire; the second as a safety net, containing at least six months' worth of income in case of job loss; the third for unexpected expenses, such as home or car repairs; and the fourth dedicated to saving for an annual vacation. The earlier we decide to be disciplined in all areas of life, including our finances, the sooner we will begin to live a fulfilled life with unlimited choices.

# CHAPTER 9 · LIFE LESSON #9

Here is a list of financial suggestions:
1. Draft your income statement, using the sample in the game CashFlow.
2. Develop income streams that surpass your total expenses. Joining a reputable network marketing business can offer invaluable education.
3. Hire a reputable financial planner and invest in companies that you use. Be sure to purchase life insurance.
4. Steer clear of unnecessary purchases ("doodads") you can't afford to pay for with cash. Prioritize paying off any high-interest debt as quickly as possible.
5. Let your assets pay for your luxuries. Starting with a duplex as an investment can fund further assets.
6. Compile a list of business ideas that solve significant life challenges.
7. Build a supportive network to foster the development of these ventures.
8. Establish a business entity and a trust to safeguard your assets.
9. Embrace your aspirations, recognizing that the journey itself is the reward.
10. Consistently work towards enhancing your net worth. Finished never is.

**LIFE LESSON #9:**
Stick To A Strong Financial Plan

**AFFIRMATION #9:**
My wealth is infinite.

# LIFE LESSON #10:

## *DEVELOP A WINNING MINDSET*

The quality of our lives is shaped by our thoughts and the subsequent actions we take towards achieving our goals. Our mindset, influenced by our perception of the world around us, is molded by our life experiences. Essentially, our lives reflect our exposures and the beliefs we've formed through personal encounters.

It is fascinating how siblings, despite being raised in the same household by the same parents, can develop vastly different mindsets, values, beliefs, and career trajectories. While numerous theories attempt to explain these differences, my focus is on sharing the steps I've taken and observed that fostered a mindset of abundance.

Just as a bodybuilder shapes their physique through a disciplined diet and workout regimen, the mind can be trained to create thoughts conducive to making decisions and taking actions that lead to success. A prime advantage of joining a high-quality network marketing company is its focus on personal growth and self-development. One of my mentors describes network marketing as a self-improvement course with a compensation plan attached to it. This is because as individuals enhance their mindset and take necessary actions, they achieve greater success in both business and life. The network marketing industry is renowned for housing some of the most positive and productive individuals, thanks to its emphasis on personal development. To cultivate a champion's mindset, here are the steps you can follow.

# CHAPTER 10 · LIFE LESSON #10

Consistently read and listen to books, applying the lessons learned and sharing those insights with others. This practice cultivates a winning attitude. Below is a list of books that I recommend for anyone looking to develop a mindset geared towards success:

- *Think and Grow Rich* by Napoleon Hill
- *How to Win Friends and Influence People* by Dale Carnegie
- *Failing Forward* by John C. Maxwell
- *Rich Dad Poor Dad* by Robert Kiyosaki
- *The Cashflow Quadrant* by Robert Kiyosaki
- *The Magic of Thinking Big* by David Schwartz
- *The Dream Giver* by Bruce Wilkinson
- *Who Moved My Cheese?* by Spencer Johnson
- *Out of the Maze* by Spencer Johnson
- *Copycat Marketing 101* by Burke Hedges

*Think and Grow Rich* guides you on what to do and how to achieve success, starting with the foundational principle that everything begins with a thought. Learning to program your mind for productive thinking is the initial step towards crafting the life you want.

*How to Win Friends and Influence People* is crucial because it teaches the art of becoming likable and trustworthy—key qualities since people prefer doing business with those they know, like, and trust. This book teaches us how to enhance personal relationships by mastering how to interact with others according to their preferences.

*Failing Forward* shifts the perspective on failure, illustrating that major achievements often follow numerous setbacks. Contrary to the school-taught fear of failure, this book highlights the importance of resilience. By examining the lives of successful individuals, we learn that their paths were paved with failures. Remember, when you are a responsible adult the opinion of other people does not matter as you are pursuing your purpose.

# CHAPTER 10 · LIFE LESSON #10

*Rich Dad Poor Dad* narrates the tale of a boy mentored by two fathers: one, a millionaire with an eighth-grade education, and the other, a university professor leading a conventional life. The story unfolds valuable lessons from both perspectives.

*The Cash Flow Quadrant* reveals the distinct mindset between wealth creators and those who aren't. The author outlines strategies for moving towards the wealthier quadrants.

*The Magic of Thinking Big* powerfully argues that thinking big requires no more effort than thinking small, emphasizing that our thoughts are a matter of choice.

*The Dream Giver* guides us through the journey of pursuing a dream, confronting the inevitable obstacles, and the importance of perseverance in living an extraordinary life.

*Who Moved My Cheese?* offers a parable on adapting to change versus being overwhelmed by it, highlighting the significance of our choices and decisions.

*Out of the Maze,* the sequel to *Who Moved My Cheese?*, follows a character overcoming fear through action, leading to unexpected discoveries.

*Copycat Marketing 101* discusses the importance of replicating successful systems for success, rather than only emulating systems designed to produce factory workers and soldiers.

Surround yourself with individuals who inspire growth and cultivate a positive, productive mindset. The adage "Birds of a feather flock together" holds more truth than just being a catchy phrase. Who are the five people you spend the most time with? Now, calculate the average of their incomes; you might find that the answer mirrors your own. To elevate your worth, seek out those who have achieved what you aspire to, learn from their path, and emulate their strategies for success.

## CHAPTER 10 · LIFE LESSON #10

You might be blessed to have personal mentors, if so commit to being coachable. You will discover mentors from afar by reading, or by watching films based on true stories to formulate your action plan. Alternatively, you could combine these methods. Essentially, the information you need is accessible; it's your responsibility to seek it out and commit to the mental and physical work required to achieve your goals.

One of my favorite inspirational films is The Pursuit of Happyness starring Will Smith, which tells the true story of a man navigating through personal and financial adversity. After his wife leaves him, he and his young son face eviction, often relying on homeless shelters for refuge, sometimes without any shelter at all. An encounter with a wealthy business man who owned a luxury sports car, prompts Will to inquire about the business man's profession. Learning the answer, Will dedicates himself to transforming his circumstances. The moral of the story lies in the power of perseverance, belief, consistency, and focused effort. It teaches us that such qualities often lead to success. Surround yourself with a supportive community and then do the following:

Turn off the television, often referred to as an electronic income reducer, and focus on creating your success story.

Disengage from the news, which typically cycles through weather updates (easily checked on your phone), reports of violence, and fluctuating economic conditions, rarely broadcasting uplifting stories.

Consciously, speak and think only of the outcomes you wish to manifest.

If you believe in a higher power, as I do in God, pray with gratitude and faith. Express thanks for your blessings, the opportunities available to you, and the good yet to come. Faith, as described in Hebrews 11:1, is "the substance of things hoped for, the evidence of things not seen." Doubt and fear have no place in effective prayer. Maintain faith, give thanks with great expectation, and take the steps necessary to realize your aspirations.

# CHAPTER 10 · LIFE LESSON #10

**Affirm.** Affirm your ideal life by asserting beliefs as though they are already true. Declare your identity, capabilities, and desires as existing realities. Examples include: "I am wealthy," "I am healthy," "I am love," "I am a billionaire," "I am enough," "I create," "I attract success," "My life is abundant," "I am patient," "I am kind," "I am disciplined," "I am consistent," "I am deserving," "I am a leader," "I am a champion," "I am the best of the best," "I am intelligent," "I am unique." Affirm these truths often throughout the day. Condition yourself to express desires through your words, as they shape your beliefs. Through repetition, you will solidify these beliefs, making it crucial to continually affirm your aspirations as if they already exist.

**Meditate.** Meditation involves closing your eyes, focusing on your breath, and clearing your mind. I enhanced my meditation practice using the Oprah and Deepak 21-Day Meditation Experience app. With a clear mind, you can then direct your focus intentionally. Repeating this process conditions your mind, transforming your mental landscape. From birth, our thoughts and beliefs are shaped by family, friends, community, church, school, television, music, social media, the news, and other influences we regularly engage with. Embracing personal evolution requires effort, notably through meditation. This practice aids in discarding disempowering thoughts to pave the way for empowering ones.

**Journal.** Journaling is highly regarded by mental health professionals as a key tool for achieving a clear mind and a more fulfilling life. It allows us to explore our desires and priorities more deeply. A journal can act as a personal diary, chronicling life events and potentially becoming a valuable family heirloom. It's also a space for creativity, where ideas for movies, books, plays, songs, and poetry can emerge. Journaling can be tailored to specific needs, such as tracking exercise routines, dietary habits, or daily steps. For business owners, maintaining a journal to organize business expenses can be beneficial. Traders might find it essential to keep a detailed journal documenting their trading activities, including wins, losses, and the timing of trades, to develop a successful trading strategy.

**Set Goals.** Goal-setting serves as a compelling reason to journal. It involves outlining both short-term and long-term objectives, spanning professional achievements, personal development, spiritual growth, and physical well-being. Financial ambitions, vacation plans, preferences for future vehicles or homes, and even wardrobe aspirations are all part of the goal-setting process. Essentially, setting goals mean planning your future in advance, a crucial practice to apply in every facet of life.

**Visualize.** Visualize by forming a vivid mental image of your goals. The mind does not distinguish between what's real and what's imagined, meaning every creation or achievement begins as an idea. Everything, from the chair you sit on to the pages you read, started as a thought. When visualizing, aim to make the scenario as lifelike as possible.

Engage in this visualization exercise. After reading these instructions, close your eyes and picture yourself at your kitchen counter, holding a knife, ready to slice a lemon in half. Consider the weight of the knife. Listen for any background sounds. Visualize the lemon resting on a white marble countertop, placed on a wooden cutting board. As you cut the lemon, think about its scent. Squeeze some juice into a cup and imagine tasting it. Is it sour? Notice your mouth's reaction to the juice. By vividly imagining every detail and engaging all your senses, your body reacts as though you are genuinely cutting, smelling, and tasting the lemon. This demonstrates the power of visualization. The clearer and more detailed your visualization, complemented by taking necessary steps, the closer you are to realizing your desires.

Remember, every creation begins with a thought, making the right mindset the foundation of any significant achievement.

# CHAPTER 10 · LIFE LESSON #10

*Which book from the list will you delve into this month?*



*Identify a successful individual you can invite for lunch or coffee. Offer to treat them as you seek their wisdom to enrich your mindset through an insightful conversation.*


Integrate a simple gratitude prayer into your daily routine. I practice T.A.G., expressing that I am Thankful, Appreciative, and Grateful for all things, a lesson imparted by one of my dearest mentors, Dr. Craig Bythewood may he rest in peace.


Develop 5 daily affirmations to bolster your mindset:
1.
2.
3.
4.
5.

*Pause for a moment to vividly imagine one thing you deeply desire to manifest. Envision it in great detail, then bring that vision to life by creating a personal vision board.*

*Each morning, before rising, dedicate five minutes to meditation.*

*Today, start a journal, focusing on what matters most to you.*

# CHAPTER 10 · LIFE LESSON #10

As we age, life's complexities increase, leading many to complicate their lives with decisions based on fleeting emotions rather than wisdom. This often stems from a lack of a straightforward, comprehensible system for achieving a fulfilling life. These 10 life lessons are intended to guide you on your path of constant and never ending improvement. Let's embrace the K.I.S.S. (Keeping life Super Simple) principle for a future filled with peace fulfillment love and joy.

Thank you for taking the time to read this book. I sincerely appreciate you investing your time with me. Refer back to this book daily and apply the simple lessons that will help you design the life you truly desire.

**Smooches!**


**LIFE LESSON #10:**
Develop a Winning Mindset

**AFFIRMATION # 10:**
All I do is WIN!!

# NOTE

# NOTE

# NOTE

# NOTE

# NOTE

After reading this book my hope is that you walk away with the understanding that simplicity leads to joy; complication leads to despair. When we become aware of our core values, our likes, our dislikes and our infinite value we can then decide to make decisions that make our souls smile.

One of my favorite quotes is, "there is a huge difference between showing up to play and preparing to win."

The content of this book will help prepare those who are ready to have a winning life .

#letswintogether

Reach out for speaking engagements and workshops: drt@simplydrt.com

For more information visit: simplydrt.com